RULES OF LIFE

RULES OF LIFE

A PERSONAL ANTHOLOGY

JULIAN FANE

Hamish Hamilton and St George's Press

First published in Great Britain 1987
by Hamish Hamilton Ltd and St George's Press
27 Wrights Lane, London w8 5TZ

British Library Cataloguing in Publication Data
Rules of life.
1. Literature—Collections
I. Fane, Julian
808.8   PN6014

ISBN 0-241-12235-X

Typeset by Rowland Phototypesetting Ltd
Bury St Edmunds, Suffolk
Printed in Great Britain by
St Edmundsbury Press Ltd
Bury St Edmunds, Suffolk
Bound by Hunter & Foulis, Scotland

I was in love with books when I was young. I still am, if less impatiently and perhaps more discreetly. Anyway, here is part of the harvest of my lifetime of reading, thoughts beautiful, inspiring, constructive, provocative, happy and sad, but all wittily brief, from the great literature of the world. Certain items I was given by or begged or borrowed from friends, who were not always able to tell me the names of the relevant authors: I apologise for these omissions. Information about sources that I can and do provide I keep to a minimum on purpose: in theory so as to allow the ideas to flow unchecked. And I confine my comments to the headings of the twelve sections, since the collection must speak for itself, although I would justify so many references to art in general by citing G. K. Chesterton: 'Every man is a special sort of artist.' The title *Rules of Life* refers more to my epigraph, the wonderful final sentences of Tolstoy's *Youth*, than to any specific design for living constructed from quotations. At the same time I hope this book is not only entertaining but useful, fun to dip into and a wise companion and guide.

Julian Fane
Lewes, Sussex, 1987

I thought and thought, and finally, late one evening, as I was sitting downstairs all alone listening to Avdotya Vasilyevna's waltz, I suddenly sprang to my feet, ran upstairs, took out the notebook on which was written 'Rules of Life', opened it, and was overcome by repentance . . . I wept – but no longer tears of despair . . . I resolved once more to write down rules of life, and was firmly convinced I should never do anything bad again, never spend a moment idly, and never break my rules.

Tolstoy, Youth

CONTENTS

ART

Are you evil, or good?

Alexander Blok, To the Muse

You reproach me for speaking of art with you, 'as though we had nothing more important in common'! Am I to gather you are in the habit of speaking of art with people you care nothing about? For you the subject of art is of minor importance, a kind of entertainment, something between politics and the day's news. Not for me! . . . What is worth discussing except art? But who is there to discuss art with? The first person who comes along? You are luckier than I, if such is the case with you, for I never meet anyone with whom I can discuss it.

Flaubert in a letter to Louise Colet

For art precedes philosophy and even science . . . And it is in this way that art is the pioneer of knowledge: those predilections of the artist he knows not why, those irrational acceptations and recognitions, reclaim, out of the world that we have not yet realised, ever another and another corner; and after the facts have been thus vividly brought before us and have had time to settle and arrange themselves in our minds, some day there will be found the man of science to stand up and give the explanation.

Robert Louis Stevenson

Yes, personally speaking too, art heightens life. She gives deeper joy, she consumes more swiftly. She engraves adventures of the spirit and the mind in the faces of her votaries; let them lead outwardly a life of the most cloistered calm, she will in the end produce in them a fastidiousness, an over-refinement, a nervous fever and exhaustion, such as a career of extravagant passions and pleasures can hardly show.

Thomas Mann, Death in Venice

Books and reality and art are alike to me.

Vincent van Gogh, Letters

The feeling for the things themselves, for reality, is more important than the feeling for pictures.

Vincent van Gogh, Letters

As for his correspondent's claim that it was the duty of literature to 'dig for the pearl in the dunghill', that, as Chekhov contended, meant disowning literature itself. For literature, he wrote, is a creative art just because it shows us life as it is. Its purpose is absolute and honest truth, and to narrow down its functions to such a specialised field as the extraction of 'pearls' is as fatal as, for instance, compelling Levitan to paint a tree without showing its dirty bark and yellow leaves. Chekhov was ready to admit that the pearl was an excellent thing in itself, but a writer, he insisted, is not a confectioner, a cosmetician or an entertainer. He is a man who has to fulfil certain duties; he is a man who has entered into a contract with his conscience and his sense of duty, and however much he may hate it, he must overcome his fastidiousness and soil his imagination with the dirt of life . . . A writer must be as objective as a chemist. He must renounce every subjective attitude to life and realise that dunghills play a very honourable part in the landscape and that vicious passions are as much a part of life as virtuous ones.

David Magarshack

All works of art whose function it is to express the soul and the emotions are always so ugly as to be beautiful, and so beautiful as to be ugly – that is a law. Their beauty is not fleshly beauty which is merely insipid, but the beauty of the spirit.

Thomas Mann, The Magic Mountain

The theatre of youth! Yet its task is a hard one. Youth is a matter of spirit, not of age. The future cannot be adequately prepared for unless the past has been thoroughly assimilated. There is no daring without humility. One is modern in one's turn of mind and not in one's allegiances. To set out merely to shock is a false posture.

Jean-Louis Barrault

One must not write except when one has things to say that are either great or profoundly beautiful; but in this case one must say them with the utmost possible simplicity, as if one were striving to prevent them from being noticed . . . It is the opposite of what is done by all the poets of this century, but it is what is done by all great men.

Stendhal

To write for the sake of writing is a crime in a man of my years and experience.

William Morris

I do not consider egotism and foul actions to be culture.

Nijinsky

Egotism, if sincere, is a manner of depicting the human heart.

Stendhal

It is wrong to think that feeling is everything. In the arts, it is nothing without form.

Flaubert

All art is, up to a point, based upon the acceptance of a convention.

Aubrey de Selincourt

Nothing is more liberating to the individual genius of an artist than the necessity of working within an accepted convention.

Aubrey de Selincourt

Tell Arnold Bennett that all rules of construction hold good only for novels which are copies of other novels. A book which is not a copy of other books has its own construction, and what he calls faults, he being an old imitator, I call characteristics.

D. H. Lawrence

Literate people appropriate all the best things they can find in books, and dress themselves in them just as certain crabs are supposed to beautify themselves with seaweed.

Saul Bellow

Every man's work, whether it be literature or music or pictures or architecture or anything else, is always a portrait of himself, and the more he tries to conceal himself the more clearly will his character appear in spite of him.

Samuel Butler

I was thinking . . . about my book, and it would not even be true to say I was thinking of those who would read it as my readers. For they would not be my readers but the readers of themselves. I should ask neither their praise nor their blame but only that they should tell me if it was right or not.

Proust

When an artist has the misfortune to be carried away by the emotion he seeks to express, he cannot express it, because he has become the thing itself instead of being its agent. Art proceeds from the brain, not the heart.

Balzac

Art is the transmission of the association of ideas.

Albert Schweitzer

The lessons which are one's apprenticeship as a man of letters . . . What it is necessary to extract and bring to light are our sentiments, our passions, which are the sentiments and passions of all men. A woman we need makes us suffer, forces from us a series of sentiments, deeper and more vital than our responses to a superior type of man who interests us . . . A writer need have no fear of undertaking a long labour. Let the intellect get to work; in the course of it there will be more than enough sorrows to enable him to finish it. Happiness serves hardly any other purpose than to make unhappiness possible. When we are happy, we have to form very tender and strong links of confidence and attachment for their rupture to cause us the precious shattering called misery. The happy years are those that are wasted; we must wait for suffering to drive us to work.

Proust

To turn to the works, I admire them; but they excite no feeling, and they leave no love.

Byron about Maria Edgeworth's books

Being impressed, in art, is worth nothing unless it yields at once to emotion; and most often it stands in the way of emotion.

Gide

The fact is that people can only react to the emotions expressed in a work of art according to their own capacity to feel those emotions.

Unknown

Only songs without words are clear to the heart.

Alexander Blok

A work of art is good if it has grown out of necessity. In this manner of its origin lies its true estimate: there is no other.

Rilke

All work that is worth anything is done in faith.

Albert Schweitzer

Faith is love of the invisible, trust in the impossible, in the improbable.

Goethe

Faith is made of confidence in God and renunciation of self.

Gide

I believe only where I pay dearly.

Georges Bernanos

By God's help I will not sell His precious gift of art for money, no, nor for fame either.

Samuel Palmer

Nobody can advise and help you, nobody. There is only one means: go inside yourself. Discover the motive that bids you write; examine whether it sends its roots down to the deepest places of your heart, confess to yourself whether you would die if writing were denied you.

Rilke

The wonderful revolution effected by Christianity consists in having said: the kingdom of God is within you. Happy paganism saw no enemy that was not outside man.

Gide

The most important factor of the development of a real composer is not the effect of the outer world on him, but the mysterious hidden permutations and combinations of what we call an internal chemistry. It is so indeed in all really vital matters of the intellect or of what we call the soul.

Ernest Newman

Perhaps it will turn out that you are called to be an artist. Then take your fate upon yourself and bear it, its burden and its greatness, without ever asking for that reward which might come from without. For the creator must be a world for himself, and find everything within himself, and in nature to which he has attached himself.

Rilke

What I have come to like best in the whole of Russian literature is the childlike Russian quality of Pushkin and Chekhov, their shy unconcern with such high-sounding matters as the ultimate purpose of mankind or their own salvation. It isn't that they did not think about these things, and to good effect, but they always felt that such important matters were not for them. While Gogol, Tolstoy and Dostoievsky worried and looked for the meaning of life and prepared for death and drew up balance-sheets, these two were distracted, right up to the end of their lives, by the current individual tasks imposed on them by their vocation as writers, and in the course of fulfilling these tasks they lived their lives quietly, treating both their lives and their work as private individual matters, of no concern to anyone else.

Pasternak

One must work, if not from inclination, at least from despair, since, as I have fully proved, to work is less wearisome than to amuse oneself.

Baudelaire

The art of living is harder than the art of writing.

Aldous Huxley

GENIUS

To carry on the feelings of childhood into the powers of manhood; to combine the child's sense of wonder and novelty with the appearances which every day perhaps for forty years has rendered familiar . . . this is the character and privilege of genius.

Coleridge

Poetical abilities require not age to mature them.

Dr Johnson to Fanny Burney

I have no faith in that class of child mind which announces an exceptional being. All the bad painters I have known have done amazing things, announcing genius, about the age of eight or ten. Alas! nothing announces genius; perhaps stubborn persistence may be a sign.

Stendhal, The Life of Henry Brulard

Perhaps the subordination of sensibility to truth and statement is ultimately a sign of genius, of the force of art overcoming a personal compassion.

Proust

The men who produce works of genius are not those who live in the most delicate atmosphere, whose conversation is most brilliant or their culture broadest, but those who have had the power, ceasing in a moment to live only for themselves, to make use of their personality as of a mirror, in such a way that their life, however unimportant it may be socially, and even in a sense intellectually, is reflected by it, genius consisting in the reflective power of the writer and not in the intrinsic quality of the scene reflected.

Proust

Genius is but a greater aptitude for patience.

Gide quoting Buffon, Journals

Even more than by what they had in common, they were united by what separated them from the rest of the world. They were both equally repelled by what was tragically typical of modern man, his shrill text-book admirations, his forced enthusiasms, and the deadly dullness conscientiously preached and practised by countless workers in the field of art and science in order that genius should remain extremely rare.

Pasternak, Dr Zhivago

She did not know, poor woman, that the true greatness wears an invisible cloak, under cover of which it goes in and out among men without being suspected; and if its cloak does not conceal it from itself always, and from all others for many years, its greatness will ere long shrink to very ordinary dimensions.

Samuel Butler, The Way of All Flesh

ARTISTS

Early could be seen in him that sign of grace which
is vouchsafed to few, whether for woe or bliss I
know not, but certainly for being apart from the
crowd.

Herzen, Memoirs

Where the historian is the man of discriminating
intelligence, the artist is the man of love.

Fürtwangler, Concerning Music

The artist always feels at his best and at the same
time most inspired where he is esteemed or even
over-esteemed. Art always reaches its peak where it
becomes the life-interest of a people.

Stefan Zweig, The World of Yesterday

Every great work of art, like every great idea, needs
an atmosphere of enthusiasm for the revelation of
its perfect beauty.

Albert Schweitzer

If, among her artists, Greece does not count a

single Spartan, is this not because Sparta threw her puny children into the pit?

Gide, Journals

The poet is always much smaller and weaker than the social average. Therefore he feels the burden of earthly existence much more intensely and strongly than other men. For him personally his song is only a scream.

Kafka

He worked, not like a man who works that he may live; but as one who is bent on doing nothing but work; having no regard for himself as a human being but only as a creator; moving about grey and unobtrusive among his fellows like an actor without his make-up, who counts for nothing as soon as he stops representing something else. He worked withdrawn out of sight and sound of the small fry, for whom he felt nothing but contempt, because to them a talent was a social asset like another; who, whether they were poor or not, went about ostentatiously shabby or else flaunted startling cravats, all the time taking jolly good care to amuse themselves, to be artistic and charming without the smallest notion of the fact that good work only comes out under pressure of a bad life; that one must die to life in order to be utterly a creator.

Thomas Mann, Tonio Kroger

In his wretched cork-lined chamber which he only left occasionally at night, this strange soothsayer [Proust] must have seen life pass unceasingly before him, wide open like a gigantic hand whose lines he understood so thoroughly in all essentials that they could not bring him any more surprises – only unending tasks every day! – How one must love work when one has got that far!

Rilke

Even the most corrupt of men, if he creates a work of art, paints into it the most perfect virtue and sensibility.

Stendhal in a letter to his sister Pauline

Beware of artistic protestations: the real artist does not wear a red waistcoat and is not eager to talk of his art.

Gide, Journals

My impression was that nobody knew he was a poet. Save for some snatches of conversation between him and Captain Somerville M.C., company commander in Corbie in September 1918, in which the names Sassoon, Nation, Athenaeum were mentioned, I personally never dreamt of it.

Lt Foulkes writing about Wilfred Owen

You have talent – which is the equivalent of a soldier having the right physical qualifications for entering West Point.

Scott Fitzgerald to a young writer

As to your thinking I should not want to be among the mediocre artists, what shall I say? It quite depends on what you call mediocre. I shall do what I can, but I do not at all despise *mediocre* in its simple sense. And one certainly does not rise above the mark by despising what is mediocre. In my opinion one must at least begin by having some respect for the mediocre, and know that it already means something and is only reached with great difficulty.

Vincent van Gogh, Letters

I perceived that to express those opinions, to write that essential book, which is the only true one, a great writer does not, in the current meaning of the word, invent it, but, since it already exists in each one of us, interpret it. The duty and the task of a writer are those of an interpreter.

Proust

Go on, don't only practise your art, but force your way into its secrets. Art deserves that, for it and knowledge can raise man to the divine. A true artist has no arrogance. He sees with regret that art is limitless. He feels darkly how far he still is from the goal; and though he may be applauded by the public, he knows with sorrow he is still far from the point where his good genius is shining like a too distant sun.

Beethoven

The way from talent to greatness is through sacrifice. What is sacrifice? I believe it is nothing else than a person's unbounded resolve, no longer limitable in any direction, to achieve his purest inward potentiality.

Rilke

1857 . . . 1864 . . . a time of deep dejection and depression, when he looked back into the pit of the misspent years, and saw so few ahead in which to redeem them. Then he composed poems which express horror of time fleeing past recall, the poems describing failures. It is a far more bitter pessimism than that of his youth. Towards the end, however, there is, in compensation, the belief in something higher than mere worldly success, a quest for moral victory, and the aim of becoming a hero and a saint. Then he sang of 'la fertilisante douleur.'

Enid Starkie, Baudelaire

It is immoral to be too good as to be too anything else . . . How often do we not see children ruined through the virtues, real or supposed, of their parents? Truly He visiteth the virtues of the fathers upon the children unto the third and fourth generation.

Samuel Butler, Notebooks

There is one word . . . which you must inscribe on your banner . . . and that word is *Loneliness*.

Logan Pearsall Smith quoting advice given him by Henry James

Therefore, dear sir, love your solitude and bear the pain that it has caused you with fair-sounding lament.

Rilke, Letters to a Young Poet

However rare and bold a thought may be, it is impossible that it should not be related to some other; and the greater an artist's solitude in his own epoch, the greater and more fecund his joy at finding relatives in the past.

Gide, Journals

It is the perpetual dread of fear, the fear of fear, that shapes the face of a brave man.

Georges Bernanos, The Diary of a Country Priest

He who desires nothing, hopes for nothing, and is afraid of nothing, cannot be an artist.

Rilke

He [William Blake] said he began them [his designs for Dante] with fear and trembling. I said, 'Oh! I have enough of fear and trembling.' 'Then,' said he, 'you'll do.'

Samuel Palmer

Courage is everything, that is, *moral courage*. External heroic courage is a trifle, often petty – but inner courage and self-reliance before a world of prejudices, one's own and other people's! . . . The much praised modesty of spirit is so seldom anything but a glorified moral cowardice.

Rahel Varnhagen

There is nothing less excusable than war and the appeal to national hatreds. But once war has come, it is both cowardly and useless to try to stand on one side under the pretext that one is not responsible. It is both impossible and immoral to judge an event from outside. One keeps the right to hold this absurd misfortune in contempt only by remaining inside it.

Albert Camus, Notebooks

Every great poet with a lively imagination is shy: in other words he is afraid of men because they can interrupt and disturb his exquisite reveries, and he trembles for his ability to concentrate. Men with their coarse pursuits come to drag him from the gardens of Armida, and thrust him into a foetid mire . . . It is because he is emotionally nourished upon reveries, and because he hates vulgarity, that a great artist is close to loving . . . The more a man has the gifts of a great artist, the more he should aspire to titles and decorations as a protective rampart against the world.

Stendhal, Love

Not having any gift whatsoever of telling stories, when I begin to tell a story aloud I am always afraid that it will be too long and that people will not listen to the end. I have often had even the mortifying experience (if, suddenly, I had to cut my story short in the middle) of waiting in vain for a voice to say: 'And so . . . ?' And perhaps indeed the lack of confidence that results from this, that fear of not being able to retain the reader's attention (even much more than my 'impatience', as has been said), is the cause of that contraction or shrinking of the end of my books. – Just a moment more, gentlemen, and I shall have finished.

Gide, Journals

The weariness which normally overtook him as he strove to give adequate expression to his vision, when he was creating original works, was absent when he was translating, for here was something that he could force himself to do, and not feel short of inspiration, or unsure of what he intended to express.

Enid Starkie, Baudelaire

Alas, Leonardo [da Vinci] will never finish anything. He thinks of the end even before he has begun.

Pope Leo X

She had gone through the crisis in the anticipation of it. That is how quick natures will often be cold and bored, or not much moved, when the positive crisis arrives.

Meredith, The Egoist

The man most subject to falling into indifference
and insensibility is the sensitive man, full of enthusiasm and mental activity. For such a man . . .
exhausts life in a moment.

Iris Origo, Leopardi

It was characteristic of Benjamin and Zélide alike
to anticipate experience. Like all swiftly reasoning
and introspective human beings they were quick to
discover a formula for their feelings and to foresee
the fatal and necessary progress of the heart.
Bruised by the past, they sought to protect themselves against the future by a vivid forecast of its
perils; thus they created and gave rein to their own
nightmares. Like children playing at ghosts, they
found themselves overtaken by the shadow of fear;
and even before the spectre had taken shape they
were in flight.

Geoffrey Scott, Portrait of Zélide

It must, however, be admitted that writers have
never been more anxious about perfection than
when . . . subordinated and modest.

Gide, Journals

Bach fought for his everyday life, but not for the
recognition of his art and of his work. In this

respect he is very different from Beethoven and Wagner, and in general from what we understand by an 'artist.' The recognition that the world gave to the master of the organ and the clavier – really only the external and contemporary side of his artistic activity – he took as a matter of course. He did not ask the world for the recognition of that part of his work that was not of his own age, and in which his deepest emotions found expression. It did not even occur to him that he could or should expect this from his epoch. He did nothing to make his Cantatas and Passion known, and nothing to perserve them. It was not his fault if they have survived to our day.

Albert Schweitzer

Somewhere some saint says to one of his penitents: Be on your guard against the pride of humility.

Gauguin, Intimate Journals

My holy of holies is . . . freedom from force and lies, whatever form the last two may take . . . I am not a liberal, a conservative, or an evolutionist, or a monk or an indifferentist. I should like to be a free artist – that is all.

David Magarshack quoting from a letter written by Chekhov

The soothing, the healing, the sacred and salutary refuge from all these vulgarities and pains is simply to lose myself in this quiet, this blessed and uninvaded workroom in the inestimable effort and refreshment of art, in resolute and beneficient production. I come back to it with a treasure of experience, of wisdom, of acquired material, of (it seems to me) seasoned fortitude and augmented capacity. Purchased by disgusts enough, it is at any rate a boon that now I hold it . . . Ah, the terrible law of the artist – the law of fructification, of fertilisation, the law by which everything is grist to his mill – the law, in short, of all acceptance of all suffering, of all life, of all suggestion and sensation and illumination. To keep at it – to strive towards the perfect, the ripe, the only best; to go on, by one's own clear light, with patience, courage and continuity, to live with the high vision and effort, to justify oneself . . . this and this alone can be my only lesson from anything . . . The consolation, the dignity, the joy of life are that discouragements and lapses, depressions and darkness come to one only as one stands without – I mean without the luminous paradise of art. As soon as I really remember it – cross the loved threshold – stand in the high chamber, and the gardens divine – the whole realm widens out again before me and around me – the air of life fills my lungs – the light of achievement flashes all over the place, and I believe, I see, I do.

Henry James, Notebooks

CRITICS

Works of art are of an infinite solitariness, and nothing is less likely to bring us near to them than criticism. Only love can apprehend and hold them, and can be just towards them.

Rilke, Letters to a Young Poet

Belinsky said that no one could understand a poet or a thinker who did not for a time become wholly immersed in his world, letting himself become dominated with his outlook, identified with his emotions, who did not in short try to live through the writer's experiences, beliefs and convictions.

Isaiah Berlin, Vissarion Belinsky

One gets to know nothing except what one loves; and the more deeply and exhaustively this knowledge is to penetrate, the more vigorous, intense and vital a love – nay, a passion – is called for.

Goethe

Thanks, Lichtenberg, thanks! – for having said that there is nothing so feeble as the conversation of learned literary men who have never thought for themselves but know a thousand historical-literary facts. It is almost like reading from a cookery book when one is hungry.

Kierkegaard, Journal

The one great argument with most people is that another should think this or that.

Samuel Butler, Notebooks

Is all thy learning nothing, unless another knows that thou knowest?

Hazlitt quoting Montaigne

There are many people who reach their conclusions of life like schoolboys; they cheat their master by copying the answer out of a book without having worked out the sum for themselves.

Kierkegaard, Journal

You will be sorry to hear I have got a physician . . . It is very odd . . . I was laughing and sitting quietly in my chair the whole time of his visit, and yet he thinks me horribly restless and irritable, and talks about my having lived *excessively* . . . which has no more to do with the malady he has to deal with than I have with the wisdom of Solomon.

Byron in a letter to Lady Melbourne

A cloud of critics, of compilers, of commentators, darkened the face of learning; and the decline of genius was soon followed by the corruption of taste.

Gibbon

The only thing that the artist cannot see is the obvious. The only thing that the public can see is the obvious. The result is the criticism of the journalist.

Oscar Wilde

The critics always think that they are cleverer than the artists. They often abuse their rights when they scold the artist for his performance. Artists are poor and tremble before the critic. They feel hurt and suffer. The soul weeps.

Nijinsky, Diary

Critics write because they need money . . . Critics work hard, but they do not really work for the sake of art. They only write about it. An artist gives all his life up to art.

Nijinsky, Diary

'I am no novel-reader; I seldom look into novels; do not imagine that I often read novels; it is really very well for a novel.' Such is the common cant. 'And what are you reading, Miss – ?' 'Oh, it is only a novel!' replies the young lady; while she lays down her book with affected indifference, or momentary shame. It is only 'Cecilia', or 'Camilla', or 'Belinda'; or, in short, some work in which the greatest powers of the mind are displayed, in which the most thorough knowledge of human nature, the happiest delineations of its varieties, the liveliest effusions of wit and humour, are conveyed to the world in the best chosen language.

Jane Austen

You spend too much time on ephemeras. The majority of modern books are merely wavering reflections of the present . . . You should read more old books . . . What is old reveals its deepest value – lastingness.

Kafka

Many a man will retract *praise*: none but a high-spirited mind will revoke its censure.

Byron, Journal

Art too is only a way of living, and one can prepare for it, living somehow, without knowing it: in everything real one is a closer nearer neighbour to it than in the unreal semi-artistic professions which, while they make show of a relatedness to art, in practice deny and attack the existence of all art, as for instance the whole of journalism does, and almost all criticism and three quarters of what calls itself and likes to be called literature.

Rilke

TRUTH

The first and last thing demanded of genius is love of truth.

Goethe

The hero of my tale – whom I love with all the power of my soul, whom I have tried to portray in all his beauty, who has been, is, and will be beautiful – is Truth.

Tolstoy, Sevastopol

Nothing is great but the true, and the smallest aspect of the true is great.

Goethe

To generalise is to be an idiot. To particularise is the alone distinction of merit. All sublimity is founded on Minute Discrimination.

William Blake's notes on Sir Joshua Reynolds' Discourses

He was a poet and hated the approximate.

Rilke

When one is honest in one's thoughts, all is true. And only in truth is health to be found. He who has not this, grows old: wrinkles do not make us old.

Rahel Varnhagen

He who is and remains honest with himself possesses the most beautiful quality of high endowment.

Goethe

To be sincere towards others one must first be sincere with oneself which is more difficult because it requires deep introspection: it is the indispensable condition of all moral development and the beginning of wisdom.

Unknown

It is useless for a man to determine first of all the outside and afterwards fundamentals. One must know oneself before knowing anything else. It is only after a man has understood himself inwardly, and has thus seen his way, that life acquires peace and significance; only then is he rid of that tiresome, ill-omened fellow traveller, the irony of life.

Kierkegaard, Journal

In order to know yourself it's necessary to have gone through frequent alternations of happiness and unhappiness, and that's something you can't give yourself.

Stendhal, Diary

A man who, night after night, falls like a lump of lead upon his bed, and ceases to live until the moment when he wakes and rises, will such a man ever dream of making, I do not say great discoveries, but even minute observations upon sleep? He barely knows that he does sleep. A little insomnia is not without its value in making us appreciate sleep, in throwing a ray of light upon that darkness. A memory without fault is not a very powerful incentive to studying the phenomena of memory.

Proust

I divide men into two lots. They are free-thinkers or they are not free-thinkers . . . Free-thinkers are those who are willing to use their minds without prejudice and without fearing to understand things that clash with their own customs, privileges, or beliefs. This state of mind is not common, but it is essential for right thinking: where it is absent discussion is apt to become more than useless. A man may be a Catholic, a Frenchman, or a Capitalist, and yet be a free-thinker: but if he put his

Catholicism, his patriotism, or his interest, above his reason, and will not give the latter free play where those subjects are touched, he is not a free-thinker. His mind is in bondage.

Tolstoy

His keen and subtle mind, deficient in those elementary feelings which are the *principles* of all moral reasonings, is better fitted for the detection of error than the establishment of truth, and his pleadings, urged or withdrawn with sceptical caution and indifference, may be employed with almost equal force as an instrument of fair argument or sophistry.

Shelley in a letter to T. Baxter, referring to a Mr Booth

If ever there lived a man of rigorous, indeed over-rigorous, and narrow principle, dominated all his life by a remorseless, never ceasing, fanatical passion for the truth, unable to compromise and adapt himself even for a short time and superficially to anything which he did not wholly and utterly believe, it was Belinsky.

Isaiah Berlin, Vissarion Belinsky

Belinsky believed that the purer the artistic impulse, the more purely artistic the work, the clearer and profounder the truth revealed.

Isaiah Berlin, Vissarion Belinsky

Every human being, no matter how miserable he may seem, has, nevertheless, his own truth. But what is the truth of others to a man who has never undertaken to discover his own?

Georges Bernanos, Joy

What constitutes the value of a man is not the truth he possesses or thinks he possesses: it is rather the sincere effort he has made to win that truth. For it is not by possession but by the pursuit of truth that man increases his power and perfects himself. If God enclosed in His right hand all of truth and in His left hand the eternal aspiration toward truth (with the certainty of never attaining it), and if He said to me: 'Choose!' I should humbly choose His left hand, saying, 'Give, Father, for pure truth is intended only for Thee.'

Gide quoting Lessing, Journals

Believe me, in art matters the saying, 'Honesty is the best policy,' is true; rather more trouble . . .

than a kind of chic to flatter the public. Sometimes in moments of worry I have longed for some of that chic, but thinking it over I say, No, let me be true to myself, and express severe, rough but true things in a rough manner. I shall not run after the art lovers or dealers; let whoever wants to come to me. In due time we shall reap, if we faint not!

Vincent van Gogh, Letters

Of course one must not extinguish one's power of imagination, but the imagination is made sharper and more correct by continually studying nature and wrestling with it.

Vincent van Gogh, Letters

Nature always begins by resisting the artist, but he who really takes it seriously does not allow that resistance to put him off his stride; on the contrary, it is that much more of a stimulus to fight for victory – and at bottom nature and a true artist agree.

Vincent van Gogh, Letters

It is true that when one loves a work one would like to do something like it, but one must sacrifice one's temporal love and not think of one's taste but of a truth which does not ask what our preferences are and forbids us to think of them.

Proust

There should always be some foundation of fact for the most airy fabric, and pure invention is but the talent of a liar.

Byron, Letter to John Murray

There is a false kind of good sense, professed by all the fools of the world, who use it to reproach people of intelligence; but there is also a true good sense which we must study because it leads to life's happiness. In general, every ill comes from ignorance of the truth, every sorrow and grief comes from expecting of men that which they are not in a condition to give you.

Stendhal in a letter to his sister Pauline

But let us never forget that not everyone who has not lost his senses thereby proves conclusively that he is in possession of them.

Kierkegaard, Journal

We all confess to the desire to get at the truth, but in

practice the desire for truth is the desire to be disillusioned.

John Macmurray, Reason and Emotion

AMBITION

The greatest human craving is the craving for
growth.

J.W.N. Sullivan, But for the Grace

I believe in that Destiny before which the ancients
bowed. Modern philosophy, with its superficial
discoveries, has infused into the heart of man a
spirit of scepticism, but I think that ere long
science will again become imaginative, and that as
we become more profound we may become also
more credulous. Destiny is our will, and our will is
our nature. The son who inherits the organisation
of the father will be doomed to the same fortunes as
his sire. All is mystery; but he is a slave who will not
struggle to penetrate the dark veil.

Disraeli, Contarini Fleming

You wish me to be frank? Very well, I will then.
One day, our day together in Nantes under the
trees, you told me you would not exchange your
happiness for the fame of Corneille. If you knew
how those words shocked me, how they chilled the
very marrow of my bones! The fame of Corneille

43

indeed! But to *be* Corneille! To feel *oneself* Corneille!

Will power, he said, was not a thing one could suddenly decree oneself to possess. It must be built up imperceptibly and laboriously out of a succession of small efforts to meet definite objects, out of a facing of daily difficulties instead of cleverly eluding them, or shifting their burden on others. The making of the substance called character was a process about as slow and arduous as the building of the Pyramids.

Edith Wharton, The Glimpses of the Moon

It is not only true that music needs to be more than itself if it is to mean anything, but that everything in the world must surpass itself in order to be itself. There must be something limitless in a human being and in his artistry for either to have definition and character.

Pasternak, Essay in Autobiography

There is a universe, in it we develop. And it matters not at all what fate is ours, when we have arrived at the perception that development *is* our fate.

Rahel Varnhagen

No one will understand me or my work unless they bear in mind that I was an unusually slow and late grower. I have not developed into much, but I have developed into much more than as a young or middle-aged man I seemed likely to do.

Samuel Butler, The Way of All Flesh

The only excuse I can make for him is that he was very young – not yet four and twenty – and that in mind as in body, like most of those who in the end come to think for themselves, he was a slow grower.

Samuel Butler, The Way of All Flesh

What one learns from personal experience is not learned so quickly, but it is imprinted more deeply on the mind.

Vincent van Gogh, Letters

To the relatively poor (who are so much worse off than the poor absolutely) education is in most cases a mocking cruelty.

George Gissing, New Grub Street

I remained alone with darkness,
The impossible became possible,

But the possible became – a dream.

Alexander Blok

Could it be that there is something dubious about hope and that when hope has disappeared from a man's life his life assumes a more severe and positive character?

Benjamin Constant, Adolphe

The knowledge of life which we grown-ups have to pass on to the younger generation will not be expressed thus: 'Reality will soon give way before your ideals,' but: 'Grow into your ideals, so that life can never rob you of them.'

Albert Schweitzer

There is nothing so bad for man or woman as to live always with their inferiors. It is a truth so important, that one might well wish to turn aside a moment and urge it – even in its lower aspects, upon the young people who are just making their associations and friendships. Many a temptation of laziness or pride induces us to draw towards those who do not know as much, or are not in some way as strong as we are. It is a smaller tax upon our powers to be in their society. But it is bad for us. I am sure I have known men, intellectually and morally very strong, the whole development of whose intellectual and moral life has suffered and been dwarfed, because they have not mixed with men greater than themselves. Whatever else they lose – they surely must lose some culture of humility. If I could choose a young man's companions, some should be weaker than himself, that he might learn patience and charity; many should be as nearly as possible his equals, that he might have the full freedom of friendship; but most should be stronger than he was, that he might for ever be thinking humbly of himself and be tempted to higher things.

Phillips Brooks

The only principle I can see in this life, is that one *must* forfeit the less for the greater.

D. H. Lawrence, Letters

All living, all doing, all artistic creation presupposes craftsmanship which can be acquired only by self-limitation.

Goethe

Woe to him who says all he could say on any subject.

Byron quoting Voltaire, Letters

Extreme busyness, whether at school or college, kirk or market, is a symptom of deficient vitality: and a faculty for idleness implies a catholic appetite and a strong sense of personal identity. There is a sort of dead-alive hackneyed people about, who are scarcely conscious of living except in the exercise of some conventional occupation . . . and they pass those hours in a sort of coma, that are not dedicated to furious moiling in the gold mill.

Robert Louis Stevenson, Virginibus Puerisque

Don't exhaust yourself too much: it is immoral.

D. H. Lawrence, Letters

You must take better care of yourself. Good health is not a personal possession . . . It is property on loan, a grace . . . I am the only son of fairly prosperous parents and believe that life is something which comes naturally to one. And so by illness I am perpetually reminded of the full extent of my frailty and therefore of the miracle of life . . . Illness gives us the possibility of protecting ourselves.

Kafka

He only earns his freedom and existence, who daily conquers them anew.

Goethe

Prayer: Do not punish me through my Mother and do not punish my Mother on my behalf – I entrust to your keeping the souls of my Father and of Mariette – give me the strength immediately to perform my daily task and thus to become a hero and a saint.

Baudelaire

Only the best people are punctual. Only the best know that even the most highly purified earthly existence is subject to conditions and cannot be carried on without the greatest regularity in the ordering of the commonest things around us, and that only by this can time be economised, which we can never recall.

Rahel Varnhagen

The human plagiarism which is most difficult to avoid for individuals (and even for nations which persevere in their faults and continue to aggravate them) is the plagiarism of oneself.

Proust

SUCCESS

There are tremendous geniuses who have but one defect, one vice – that of being especially appreciated by the vulgar, by people susceptible to cheap poetry . . . Popularity which seems to give genius greater scope actually vulgarises it; authentic beauty is not for the masses. For my own consumption I prefer geniuses a little less agreeable to the touch, more haughty in their manner and their tastes, more reserved.

Flaubert, Letters

Expressionist art involves a dangerous tension of the spirit. But the frenzied writhings, the Catherine-wheel convolutions of van Gogh are further out of control than anything in El Greco, and are in fact painfully similar to the paintings of actual madmen. Perhaps that is one reason why they have proved so popular. The assault they make on our feelings is so violent that people who are not normally moved recognise that something unusual is going on. Those to whom the rhythms of a Seurat would be as inaudible as the music of the spheres, cannot fail to hear the voice of van Gogh rising to a scream of rapture, pity or despair.

Kenneth Clark, Landscape into Art

Both Gordon and Dudorov moved in good uni-
versity circles, they spent their lives among good
books, good thinkers, good composers and music
which was as good yesterday as today (but always
good!) and they did not know that the misfortune
of having average taste is a great deal worse than
having no taste at all.

Pasternak, Dr Zhivago

I find more and more that it is well to be on the side
of the minority, since it is always the more intelli-
gent.

Goethe

Nothing is more odious than the majority. For it
consists of a few vigorous pacemakers, of rascals
who accommodate themselves, of weaklings who
follow suit, and of the multitude that trots after
without knowing in the slightest what it wants.

Goethe

No man on earth who conscientiously opposes you
or any other organised democracy, and flatly pre-
vents a great many wrongs and illegalities from
taking place in the state to which he belongs, can
possibly escape with his life. The true champion of

justice, if he intends to survive for even a short time, must necessarily confine himself to private life and leave politics alone.

Plato, Socrates' Apology

Plato's direction of thought was towards the establishing of two worlds; the world of appearance (or of Opinion) in which the ignorant are content to live, and the spiritual world (the world of Knowledge) which is the only home of the wise.

Aubrey de Selincourt

There is in true beauty something which vulgar souls cannot admire.

Congreve

Vulgarity, by extinguishing imagination, has the immediate effect of boring me to death.

Stendhal, Love

All forms of expression hide within them the seeds of their own destruction, and just as classicism tends to emptiness and lack of vitality, so naturalism tends to vulgarity. It is the popular style, the style that can be understood without effort or education; and as with all forms of luxury, the saving of intellectual and spiritual effort creates an insatiable appetite for more.

Kenneth Clark, Landscape into Art

You cannot imagine an author so great that his most banal qualities are not the first to be appreciated.

Gide, Journals

But why does the paper stultify its earlier articles by advertising 'Best Sellers'? Of all marks of the unliterary journal this is the clearest. If the Canadian Bookman were to take a new line and advertise eulogistically the worst sellers, it might do something towards its object.

Thomas Hardy

I fled the crowd, despised it, but that German musician with his strong deep soul, his poetic nature, does not reject the world, does not flee the crowd. He is proud of their applause. He knows he is a mere insignificant link in the endless chain of humanity.

Goncharov, The Same Old Story

Grant me the grace, Lord God Almighty, to compose a few beautiful verses which will prove to me that I'm not the least of all men, that I'm not inferior to those whom I despise.

Baudelaire

Alas, I shall never know security, which consists in being like others.

Kierkegaard, Journal

Here is a fact one should often think of. Thackeray was thirty years preparing to write his first novel, but Dumas writes two a week.

Tolstoy, Diary

How can a writer help growing worse and destroying the finest talent, if he has the audacity to write in a single year two tragedies and a novel; and, further, when he appears to work only in order to scrape together immense sums of money? I do not blame him for trying to become rich, and to earn present renown; but if he intends to live long in futurity, he must begin to write less and to work more.

Goethe on Victor Hugo, Conversations with Eckermann

55

It is provided in the essence of things that from any fruition of success, no matter what, shall come forth something to make a greater struggle necessary.

Lewis Mumford quoting Whitman, The Condition of Man

You've got to stop worrying about successes and failures, once and for all. They are not your affair.

Chekhov in a letter to Olga Knipper

The less importance he attached to the opinion of men the more did he feel the presence of God within him.

Tolstoy, Father Sergius

More conducive to success in life than the desire for much knowledge is the being satisfied with ignorance on irrelevant subjects.

Thomas Hardy

Would you believe it that I now feel nervous – nervous of what? Of not being successful! That's the explanation of the indecision which has hampered me so often.

Baudelaire in a letter to his mother

The most lamentable victims of all are the victims of adulation. What force of character is needed to detest the things that flatter us.

Gide, The Coiners

As for fame, look I implore you at famous people; see how the waters of dullness spread around them as they enter; observe their pomposity, their prophetic airs; reflect that the greatest poets were anonymous; think how Shakespeare cared nothing for fame; how Donne tossed his poems into the wastepaper basket; write an essay giving a single instance of any modern English writer who has survived the disciples and the admiration, the autograph hunters and the interviewers, the dinners and the luncheons, the celebrations and the commemorations with which English society so effectively stops the mouths of its singers and silences their songs.

Virginia Woolf, A Letter to a Young Poet

SOCIETY

Intellectual labour tears a man out of society. A craft, on the other hand, leads him towards men.

Kafka

I must be alone with my work, and have as little need of hearing others talk of it as a man might wish to see in print, or to collect, others' opinions about the woman he loves.

Rilke, Letters

If God has given a commandment, it is this: Be solitary from time to time. For He can come only to one man, or to two whom He can no longer distinguish.

Rilke, Journal

To rejoice in one's heart and to love one needs solitude, but to be a success one must get about in society.

Stendhal, Love

Although physical pleasure, being natural, is known to all, it is only of secondary importance to sensitive, passionate people. If such people are derided in drawing-rooms or made unhappy by the intrigues of the worldly, they possess in compensation a knowledge of pleasure utterly inaccessible to those moved only by vanity or money.

Stendhal, Love

The more one pleases generally, the less one pleases profoundly.

Stendhal, Love

But only much later by experience of life did I become convinced that it is harmful to think, and still more harmful to express, much that seems very noble but ought to lie hidden in the heart of each man, and that noble words seldom go with noble deeds. I am convinced that if a good intention has been uttered, it is difficult and for the most part impossible to carry it out.

Tolstoy, Childhood, Boyhood and Youth

I get lost in conversations. Most often I derive nothing from them but dejection and bitterness. In them I compromise my inner life, everything that is best in me. In order to keep the conversation going, I throw into it my favourite thoughts, the ones to which I am most secretly and solicitously attached. My shy and awkward speech disfigures, mutilates them, throwing them out into the bright light in disorder and confusion and only half-dressed. When I go away I gather up and hug to my breast my scattered treasure, trying to put back into place dreams that are bruised like fruit fallen from the tree onto rocks.

Gide quoting Maurice de Guérin, Journals

The pleasures of high society are no pleasure at all for a happy woman.

Stendhal, Love

The more a man becomes used to pleasure and refinement the more deprivation in life he prepares for himself.

Tolstoy, Diary

The moment you enter society, you draw the key from your heart and put it in your pocket. Those who fail to do so are fools.

Goethe

You are censorious, child; when you are a little older, you will learn to dislike everybody, but abuse nobody.

Byron

It is nothing to bear the *privations* of adversity, or, more properly, ill fortune; but my pride recoils from its *indignities*.

Byron in a letter to Thomas Moore

Like most very proud persons, he chose his intimates in general from a rank beneath his own.

Thomas Moore about Byron

Wine, songs, dances, wooing, visual delights are all organic parts of a fuller life; but when they dominate life and become its sole object they lead to psychological disintegration.

Lewis Mumford, The Condition of Man

Flippancy, the most hopeless form of intellectual vice.

George Gissing, New Grub Street

I used to rely on my personality; now I know that

my personality really rested on the fiction of 'position'. Having lost my position I find my personality of no avail.

Oscar Wilde

The true snob likes a person or accepts an idea, not because the person is likeable, or because the idea seems to him to be true, but because both happen to be fashionable, and familiarity with them gives him a sense of self-satisfaction.

Unknown

Henry James had, he says in a letter to Paul Bourget, 'an inalienable mistrust of the great ones of the earth and a thorough disbelief in any security with people who have no imagination. They are the objects, not the subjects, of imagination and it is not in their compass to conceive of anything whatever. They can only lead their hard functional lives.'

Leon Edel, The Treacherous Years

What is called the opinion of society is a phantom power, yet as is often the case with phantoms, of more force over the minds of the unthinking than all the flesh and blood arguments which can be brought to bear against it. It is a combination of the many weak against the few strong; an association of the mentally lifeless to punish any manifestation of mental independence. The remedy is to make all strong enough to stand alone; and whoever has once known the pleasure of self-dependence, will be in no danger of relapsing into subserviency.

Harriet Taylor

'How do you manage, Monsieur France,' asked Proust; 'how do you manage to know so much?'
  'The answer is quite simple, my dear Marcel. When I was your age I was not, like you, good-looking: nobody, in fact, much cared for me. Consequently I was never asked out, but stayed at home reading, reading endlessly.'

Unknown

Only those who know the supremacy of the intellectual life – the life which has a seed of ennobling thought and purpose within it – can understand the grief of one who falls from that serene activity into the absorbing soul-wasting struggle with worldly annoyances.

George Eliot, Middlemarch

The world is fair.

Alexander Blok, Retribution

INFLUENCE

I am convinced that nothing has so marked an influence on the direction of a man's mind as his appearance, and not his appearance itself so much as his conviction that it is attractive or unattractive.

Tolstoy, Boyhood

One must in general be so careful with names; it is so often the name of a misdeed upon which a life is shattered, not the nameless and personal action itself, which was perhaps a quite definite necessity of that life and could be taken on by it without trouble.

Rilke

The value of our acts only exists in proportion to what we are . . . It is only what we are that has an influence.

Rahel Varnhagen

You're kind to satisfy Katherine [Mansfield] with what you could earn for her, give her; and she will only be satisfied with what you are.

D. H. Lawrence in a letter to Middleton Murry

Military life in general degrades men. It places them in conditions of complete idleness, that is, absence of all rational and useful work; frees them from their common human duties, which it replaces by merely conventional duties to the honour of the regiment, the uniform, the flag; and, while giving them on the one hand absolute power over the other men, also puts them into conditions of servile obedience to those of higher rank than themselves.

Tolstoy, Resurrection

Unfortunately, power battens on its own success and its appetite grows with every morsel it swallows.

Lewis Mumford, The Condition of Man

I only wish the ordinary people had an unlimited capacity for doing harm; then they might have an unlimited power for doing good; which would be a splendid thing were it so. Actually they have neither. They cannot make a man wise or stupid; they simply act at random.

Plato, Socrates when in prison to Crito

In matters of feeling, the public seldom rises above the level of meanness in ideas; yet women appoint the public as supreme judge of their lives. This applies even to the most distinguished women, who are often unaware of it, and even believe and declare that the contrary is true.

Stendhal, Love

It gave me great relief to talk of my disorder with Dr Johnson, and when I discovered that he himself was subject to it I felt that strange satisfaction which human nature feels at the idea of participating distress with others; and the greater person our fellow-sufferer is, so much the more good does it do us.

Boswell, London Journal

Believe me, you add to your grievance by taking it out for an airing. It is quite true that it may do good to discuss it calmly with your confessor. Or, very occasionally, it may be your duty to bring something to the notice of a person in higher authority. But to chatter and gossip over your grievances never yet did any good, never yet afforded any real relief; you only hypnotise yourself into imagining your resentment to be stronger than it really is. It is a conspiracy against your peace of mind.

Ronald Knox, The Priestly Life

Praise acts so powerfully not only on a man's feelings but also on his reason, that under its pleasant influence I felt as if I had grown much wiser, and thoughts gathered in my mind with unusual rapidity.

Tolstoy, Boyhood

If a man does not alter his views about life and art, it is because he is devoted to his own vanity rather than to the truth.

Belinsky

He who begins by loving his Christianity above truth will very shortly love his church or sect above Christianity, and will end by loving himself (his own peace of mind) above all else in the world.

Tolstoy quoting Coleridge

Vanity is a feeling quite incompatible with true sorrow, and yet that feeling is so firmly grafted into man's nature that even the deepest sorrow rarely banishes it. Vanity in sorrow expresses itself by a desire to appear either stricken with grief, or unhappy, or stoical. And these mean devices, which we do not confess, but which hardly ever leave us even in our deepest sorrow, rob it of its strength, dignity and serenity.

Tolstoy, Childhood

Sorrow never kills.

Tolstoy, Childhood

I detest that fatuity of mind which believes that what is explained is also excused; I hate that vanity which finds it interesting to describe the harm that it has done, and asks to be pitied at the end of the recital, and, as it patrols with impunity among the ruins for which it is responsible, gives to self-analysis the time which should be given to repentance.

Benjamin Constant, Adolphe

HAPPINESS

I love fun, but too much is abominable.

William Blake

I cannot endure the company of many persons, and the society of one is either great pleasure or great pain.

Shelley

The more a thing is perfect, the more it feels pleasure and likewise pain.

Unknown

If you seek happiness and beauty simultaneously, you will attain neither one nor the other, for the price of beauty is self-denial. Art, like the Jewish God, wallows in sacrifices.

Flaubert in a letter to Louise Colet

Tolstoy's uncomfortable household, the lack of ease in Rodin's rooms: it all points to the same thing – that one must decide, either this or that. Either happiness or art.

Rilke

The only definite thing is suffering.

Kafka

There is no happiness in comfort; happiness is brought by suffering. Man is not born to happiness. Man earns his happiness and always by suffering. Here there is no injustice, for life's calling and consciousness . . . is acquired by experience pro and contra which must be felt in the process of living . . . Such is the law of our planet. But this immediate consciousness, felt in the process of living, is such a great joy, for which one may pay by years of suffering.

Dostoievsky, Notes for Crime and Punishment

'Be happy' – no, that one cannot say, but 'Be gentle and yet not a weakling' – that one can say.

Tolstoy in a letter to his sister-in-law Tanya Bers

The powerful means for achieving true happiness is – and without any dogma – to spread out from oneself, in every direction, like a spider, a whole spider's web of love and to catch in it everything that comes along, whether it is an old woman, a girl or a policeman.

Tolstoy, Diary

Happiness like mockery is catching; at least none but those who are happy in themselves can make others so. No wit, no understanding, neither riches nor beauty can communicate this feeling. The happy alone can make happy; love and joy are twins born of each other.

Hazlitt

Extract from each day a maximum of beauty, make of every moment a work of art.

Unknown

Suddenly realising that death was awaiting me any hour, any minute, I decided without understanding why . . . that man cannot be happy except in making the most of the present and not thinking about the future.

Tolstoy, Youth

He who bends to himself a joy
Doth the winged life destroy;
But he who kisses the joy as it flies
Lives in Eternity's sunrise.

William Blake

Certainly flowers have the easiest time on earth.

Wilfred Owen

LOVE

Take nothing seriously, except friendship and love. All the rest is but a bad joke.

Stendhal

Do not expect love for a human being will bring you happiness. This is too serious a love. Happiness can be found more easily in action, in an absorbing work full of surprises and which leaves you no peace.

Jacques Chardonne

But it is the difficult that is enjoined upon us, almost everything serious is difficult, and everything is serious.

Rilke, Letters to a Young Poet

It is not true that love makes all things easy: it makes us choose what is difficult.

George Eliot, Felix Holt

We shouldn't feel more for people than they feel for themselves.

Henry James, A London Life

The gift for education, the gift of patient love, of complete persevering devotion is more rarely met with than any other.

Herzen, Memoirs

There is no greater folly than to seek to correct the natural infirmities of those we love.

Fielding

It seemed to me, just because Dmitri was taking Dubkhov's part so warmly, that he no longer liked or respected him, but did not admit this out of stubbornness lest anyone should accuse him of inconstancy. He was one of those men who love their friends all their lives, not so much because the friends always remain lovable to them as because, having once grown fond of anyone even under a misapprehension, they consider it dishonourable to cease to care for them.

Tolstoy, Childhood, Boyhood and Youth

There are two sides to every attachment: one loves, the other allows himself to be loved; one kisses, the other gives his cheek to be kissed . . . In our friendship it was I who kissed and Dmitri who presented his cheek; but he too was ready to kiss me. We cared for one another equally because we

76

knew and valued each other; but that did not prevent him exerting an influence on me and my submitting to him.

Tolstoy, Boyhood

The memory of our recent correspondence and your two letters have made me consider seriously our relations to each other. We have been playing at friendship. That cannot exist between two persons as disparate as we are. You, perhaps, are able to reconcile scorn for a man's convictions with a feeling of attachment for him; but I cannot do this . . . Therefore it is better for us to separate and go our own ways, respecting each other, yet making no attempt to enter into that closer relationship which can be achieved only when there is a unity of the dogmas of faiths, that is to say of fundamentals which are beyond intellectual processes. We differ entirely on these fundamentals. And I cannot hope to come round to yours because I have already had them. Nor can I hope that you will come round to mine because you have already travelled too far along your temptingly well-beaten road.

Tolstoy in a letter included in Alexandra Tolstoy's biography of her father

That is where young people so often and so grievously go wrong . . . they throw themselves at each other when love comes over them, scatter themselves abroad, just as they are in all their untidiness, disorder and confusion.

Rilke

When I saw him looking up like that I knew that I loved him, and that it was for always. It was as if my heart turned over, and I knew that it was for always. It's a strange feeling – when you know quite certainly in yourself that something is for always. It's like what death must be. All the insouciance, all the gaiety is a bluff.

Jean Rhys, Good Morning, Midnight

It never enters anyone's mind to demand of an individual that he be 'happy' – but when a man marries, people are astonished if he is not! (And besides, it is really not at all important to be happy, either as individual or as married man.)

Rilke

The aim of marriage, as I feel it, is not by means of demolition and overthrowing of all boundaries to create a hasty communion, the good marriage is rather one in which each appoints the other as guardian of his solitude and shows this greatest trust that he has to confer. A togetherness of two human beings is an impossibility and, where it does seem to exist, a limitation, or mutual compromise which robs one side or both sides of their fullest freedom and development. But, granted the consciousness that even between the closest people there persist infinite distances, a wonderful living side by side can arrive, if they succeed in loving the expanse between them.

Rilke

I should like to know *who* has been carried off except poor dear me. I have been more ravished myself than anybody since the Trojan war. I am accused of being hard on women. It may be so, but I have been their martyr. My whole life has been sacrificed *to* them and *by* them.

Byron

One must love you – and submit.

Benjamin Constant to Madame de Charriére (Zélide)

Ubu's admirable remark to Madame Ubu: 'You are very ugly today. Is it because we have guests?'

Gide quoting from Alfred Jarry's Ubu Roi

Are you prepared, and fitted, to run a household on an income of less, perhaps, than three hundred a year? Do you love me enough, and have you enough respect for my wishes and tastes, to fall in with my way of living and try to make us both as happy as you can? Are you willing to follow the plans I will draw up for the improvement of your mind, so that we can be good company for each other, and not dull, when we are alone, and neither visiting or being visited? Will you be willing to bend your inclinations according to mine – like the people whom I like, love those whom I love, and be indifferent to those to whom I am indifferent? Do you love me enough to change from a bad temper to a good one, the moment I come into a room? Is your temper sufficiently good for you to try to smooth me down when something has gone wrong and I am irritable in consequence? Will you be content and happy to live in the place to which I am sent, preferring it, because your husband is there, to courts and cities without him? I am a man with a wide knowledge of the world, and all these qualities are absolutely necessary to me in a wife. To a woman who has these qualities I shall be proud to give everything in return that is in my power, so as to make her happy. These are the questions I have always meant to ask the woman with whom I intend to pass my life: and when you can answer them satisfactorily, I shall be happy to have you in my arms, without considering in the slightest whether you are beautiful or rich.

Jonathan Swift's proposal of marriage

The plea of marriage is not a legitimate defence against love.

Who knows not how to conceal knows not how to love.

No one can surrender to two loves.

It is improper to love a woman whom one would be ashamed to desire in marriage.

Love disclosed seldom endures.

Success too easily won soon strips love of its charm; obstacles enhance its value.

Only merit is worthy to be loved.

A lover is always timorous.

True jealousy always aggravates the condition called love.

True love finds nothing good but what it knows will please its beloved.

A slight presumption leads a lover to suspect the worst of the beloved.

Stendhal quoting from a 12th century Code of Love

That two people destined to love each other shall meet is incredible. The case is so rare that one could dispense with talking about it. Yet in society everything is arranged as though exception were the rule – love shared and lasting which marriage implies. Everything is organised in favour of this marvellous exception.

Jacques Chardonne

Perseverance is the great thing in love, once it has taken hold of us. That is, if love is returned, for if it is decidedly not returned, one is literally absolutely helpless.

Vincent van Gogh

Make up your mind to this, that if a woman does not like you of her own accord, that is, from voluntary impressions, nothing you can do or say or suffer for her sake will make her, but will set her more against you.

Hazlitt

Hesitate to call forth anything except the utmost passion of a woman's heart.

Nathaniel Hawthorne

The one woman who never gives herself is your free woman, who is always giving herself.

D. H. Lawrence, Letters

No human being has the right to hold another by any power other than that person's inner necessity.

Rahel Varnhagen

How does it happen that some people fail to tie anyone to themselves, to tie themselves to anybody, while others are centres of human joys and pain and affection – why are some people like that? What makes them so? Suffering? But have I not suffered – have I not? Yet my pain was evidently vain. It never resulted in anything, but remained a pain which ate into all of my being . . . There was no other side to my suffering. Why are some women mothers and grannies to everyone? – Why do other women fail to be mothers even to the children they have borne? – What makes a heart sterile? Why does no one tell me his sorrow – what separates me from the rest of the world? Am I not kind? Is it egoism?

Unknown

She knows that she is fashioned to save life, not merely to undergo it . . . and it is only with this vital energy as the foundation of one's being that a really deep suffering is thinkable; a vital energy that rebels against its torments, that is by turns vanquished and victorious but never acknowledges pain as the meaning of life.

Rahel Varnhagen

She said that privileged souls, regal natures, long remain innocent; that they learn only with difficulty to perceive that there is such a thing as baseness, and constantly ignore this experience in the sense that they return again and again with confidence to men and life, in spite of their having neither forgotten nor avenged the wrongs they have suffered.

Unknown

Virginity of soul and impurity of body can go together.

Vincent van Gogh

There is nothing truer than that the people who have always gone right don't know half as much about the nature and ways of doing right as those who have gone wrong.

Thomas Hardy

From bad to good is not far.

Lermontov

In a passionless condition reason rules man, but when passions control him they control his reason too, and only add a more fatal boldness to his bad actions.

Tolstoy, Diary

We should do well to remember that nothing that has happened is impossible; that this is a fundamental law of history. And men and women must seem possible to themselves, for no one is a monster in his own estimation.

Edith Sichel, The Later Years of Catherine de Medici

I do not believe much in the benefits of sudden change; rather in successive reformations.

Alfred de Vigny

Rahel felt that all blows are light in comparison with that of finding oneself deceived in a person . . . Natures like Rahel's are above all exposed to this pain. For they have a boundless confidence in the nobility of others.

Ellen Key, Rahel Varnhagen

May you never again be wounded through the objects of your love – the only wounds which tell in this life. The rest are scratches.

Mrs Browning in a letter to W. W. Storey

It takes very little to bring about a woman's fall, but you have to lift a whole world in order to lift her.

Paul Gauguin, Intimate Journals

In every love there are many different loves . . . The principal thing is to continue and to persevere, he who wants variety must remain faithful. And he who wants to know many women must stick to one and the same.

Vincent van Gogh

Faithfulness is a matter of course, it is a condition of love. Without a faithful spirit one cannot love at all – cannot live, I might say: for what does one know of oneself, unless one feels oneself to be true?

Rahel Varnhagen

How intense can be the longing to escape from the emptiness and dullness of human verbosity, to take refuge in nature, apparently so inarticulate, or in the wordlessness of long grinding labour, of sound sleep, of true music, or of a human understanding rendered speechless by emotion.

Pasternak, Dr Zhivago

Talk as much as possible to women. They ask so many questions.

Disraeli

Silence is not always tact and it is tact that is golden, not silence.

Samuel Butler, Notebooks

I hold this to be the highest task for a union of two people: that one shall guard the other's solitude.

Rilke

True kindness presupposes the faculty of imagining others' suffering as one's own. I mean that without imagination there can be weakness, but not true kindness.

Gide, Journals

The majority of men are subjective towards themselves and objective towards all others, terribly objective sometimes – but the real task is in fact to be objective towards oneself and subjective towards all others.

Kierkegaard

The heart is a world of its own and must contrive its own creation and destruction.

Goethe

If we had no rivals, physical gratification would not be transformed into love, that is to say, if we had no rivals or believed we had none, for they need not actually exist. That illusory life, which our suspicion and jealousy give to rivals who have no existence, is sufficient for our good. Happiness is salutary for the body, but sorrow develops the powers of the spirit. Moreover, does it not on each occasion reveal to us a law which is no less indispensable for the purpose of bringing us back to truth, of forcing us to take things seriously by pulling up the weeds of habit, scepticism, frivolity and indifference? It is true that that truth which is incompatible with happiness, with health, is not always compatible with life itself. Sorrow ends by killing.

Proust

I believe there comes a point in love, once and no more, which later on the soul seeks – yes, seeks in vain – to surpass: I believe that happiness wears out in the effort made to recapture it; that nothing is more fatal to happiness than the remembrance of happiness.

Gide, The Immoralist

The stress of injured love is always tempted to speech which seems its contradiction.

George Gissing, New Grub Street

Without believing an instant in Albertine's love, twenty times I wanted to kill myself for her; I had ruined myself and destroyed my health for her. When it is a question of writing, we have to be scrupulous, look close and cast out what is not true.

But when it is only a question of our own lives, we ruin ourselves, make ourselves ill, kill ourselves for the sake of lies. Of a truth, it is only out of the matrix of those lies . . . that we can extract a little truth. Sorrows are obscure and hated servitors whom we cannot replace but who by strange and devious ways lead us to truth and to death. Happy those who have encountered the former before the latter and for whom, closely as one may follow the other, the hour of truth sounds before the hour of death.

Proust

As man advances through life, and begins to see things from a higher angle, then everything which the world has agreed to call beauty loses much of its importance for him, as well as carnal pleasures and other trifles of that sort. In the eyes of a clear-sighted and disillusioned man each season has its beauty, and it is not spring which is the most enchanting, nor winter the most evil. Henceforth beauty will not mean for him the promise of physical pleasure and happiness. It is Stendhal who says that beauty will henceforth be the form which seems to promise most kindliness, most loyalty in fulfilling one's share of the bargain, most honesty in keeping trust, most delicacy in intellectual perception. Ugliness will mean cruelty, avarice, falseness and stupidity.

Many men do not know these things, and only learn them later to their own cost. Just a few of us know them now, but each one of us knows them for himself alone. By what means could I ever make it clear to a young flibbertigibbet that the great attraction and sympathy I feel for ageing women, for those poor unfortunate creatures who have suffered much through their lovers, their husbands, through their children, and most of all through their own fault, are coupled with no sensual desire? If the notion of virtue and love is not mingled with our pleasures, then those pleasures will only become anguish and the source of remorse.

Baudelaire

DESTINY

'Aspirin,' Colette said, 'changes the colour of my thoughts. It makes me gloomy. I would rather suffer cheerfully.'

Maurice Goudeket

But worries like mine, and even worse than mine, do not produce in everyone the same degree of suffering. You have got to consider two entirely different things: the material fact which is the cause of the suffering and the individual's capacity for suffering which depends upon his temperament. Still I am sure there are many people who suffer as much as and more than I do and yet manage to work. Literary work constantly forces me to exploit the very feelings that are most closely connected with suffering.

Proust

Surely so delicate a mind as I have cannot be greatly blamed for wavering a little when such horrible obstacles oppose my favourite scheme.

Boswell, London Journal

I reflected upon all my mental sufferings in the last year; their cause seemed inadequate to their poignancy.

Fanny Burney

Only women and those who are slighted know how to observe, because everything touches their feelings and observation is born of wounds.

Balzac

Such is the sad destiny of tender souls: they remember their woes in the smallest detail, whereas moments of happiness throw them into such an ecstasy that they cannot remember them.

Stendhal in a letter to Madame Dembowski

I swear, gentlemen, that to be too conscious is an illness, a real thoroughgoing illness.

Dostoievsky, Notes from Underground

The partisans of socialism are people who envisage principally the urban population. They know neither the poetry nor the beauty of rural life, nor its suffering.

Tolstoy

There is nothing like *pace* to drive away unpleasant considerations.

Whyte Melville, Market Harborough

A writer compensates himself in his own fashion for the unfairness of life.

Balzac

At moments when one feels depressed without cause one must think of those who are really unhappy.

Tolstoy, Diary

I'm beginning to see that you must bother very little about the future if you want to be happy or merely reasonable.

Stendhal, Diary

Regrets, remorse, repentance, are past joys seen from behind.

Gide, The Immoralist

Death, thou makest wise the heart . . .
I understand, I understand, Isora:

The immutable law of the heart
Is that happiness and suffering are one.

Alexander Blok, The Rose and the Cross

The difference between a man who faces death for the sake of an idea and an imitator who goes in search of martyrdom is that while the former expresses his idea most fully in death, it is the strange feeling of bitterness which comes from failure that the latter really enjoys; the former rejoices in his victory, the latter in his suffering.

Kierkegaard, Journal

The more patient, quiet and open we are in our sorrowing, the more deeply and the more unhesitatingly will the new thing enter us, the better shall we deserve it, the more will it be our destiny.

Rilke

It is not so much by his acts that a lover of humanity makes himself useful as by his example. I mean by his very figure, by the image he offers and leaves behind, and by the happiness and serenity it radiates.

Gide, Journals

It is only while we are suffering that our thoughts, in a constant state of agitation and change, cause the depths within us to surge as in a tempest to a point where we see that they are subject to laws which, until then, we could not observe, because the calm of happiness left those depths undisturbed. Perhaps only in the case of a few great geniuses is it possible for this movement to be constantly felt without their suffering turmoil and sadness; but again it is not certain, when we contemplate the spacious and uniform development of their serene achievements, that we are not too much taking for granted that the buoyancy of the work implies that of its creator, who perhaps, on the contrary, was continuously unhappy.

Proust

I have said that impressionism was the painting of happiness. This, although one of its charms for us, is also one of its limitations, for the impressionists were thereby cut off from the deepest intuitions of the human spirit, and in particular from those which great artists achieve in the last years of their lives. There used to be a comfortable belief that great artists grew old in a kind of haze of benevolence, but a theory which does not apply to Dante, Shakespeare, Milton, Tolstoy, Beethoven, Michelangelo and Rembrandt is not really of much value; and the history of art shows that the minds which

97

have not simply given up the struggle end in a kind of sublime despair at the spectacle of human destiny.

Kenneth Clark, Landscape into Art

Intensity of joy involves a great expenditure of nervous energy, and in all but the most robust is balanced by equally great despair.

Kenneth Clark, Landscape into Art

I was told that when I grew older I should feel less; but I do not find it so; I am sooner, I think, hurt than ever. I suppose it is with very old age as with extreme youth, the effect of weakness; neither of those stages of life have firmness for bearing misfortunes.

Fanny Burney quoting Mrs Delany

Everything in life comes too soon or too late.

George Gissing, New Grub Street

One of the surprising and unique faculties of the Christian religion is its ability to guide and console anyone who has recourse to it in any juncture or dilemma whatsoever. If there is any remedy for the past, it prescribes and supplies it, gives the light and strength to apply it, whatever the cost: if there is none, it provides the means of carrying out in reality the proverb about making a virtue of necessity. It teaches people to pursue steadily what they have begun lightly: it inclines the mind to accept willingly what has been imposed by force, and gives to a rash but irrevocable choice all the sanctity, all the wisdom and, let us even say boldly, all the joys of a vocation. It is a path so made that by whatever labyrinth or precipice man may reach it, once he takes the first step, he can thenceforward walk safely and cheerfully along it and arrive happily at a happy end.

Manzoni, The Betrothed

To have a positive religion is not necessary. To be in harmony with oneself and the whole is what counts, and this is possible without positive and specific formulation in words.

Goethe

Religion is something infinitely simple, simple-minded! It is no knowledge, no content of feeling, it is no duty and no renunciation, it is no limitation: but in the entire expanse of the universe it is a direction of the heart.

Rilke

Christianity is certainly not melancholy, it is, on the contrary, glad tidings – for the melancholy; to the frivolous it is certainly not glad tidings, for it wishes first of all to make them serious.

Kierkegaard, Journal

Most people really believe that the Christian commandments (e.g. to love one's neighbour as oneself) are intentionally a little too severe – like putting the clock on half an hour to make sure of not being late in the morning.

Kierkegaard, Journal

The immediate person thinks and imagines that when he prays, the important thing, the thing he must concentrate upon, is that God should hear what he is praying for. And yet, in the true, eternal sense it is just the reverse: the true relation in prayer is not when God hears what is prayed for, but when the person praying continues to pray until he is the one who hears what God wills. The immediate person, therefore, makes demands in his prayer: the true man of prayer only attends.

Kierkegaard, Journal

Prayer and art are passionate acts of will.

Kafka

Indefessus favente deo – unwearied by God's favour.

Vincent van Gogh

God is wisdom; one cannot love wisdom without loving God.

Bernard Palissy

Now it is time that we were going, I to die and you to live, but which of us has the happier prospect is unknown to anyone but God.

Plato, Socrates' Apology